This belongs to

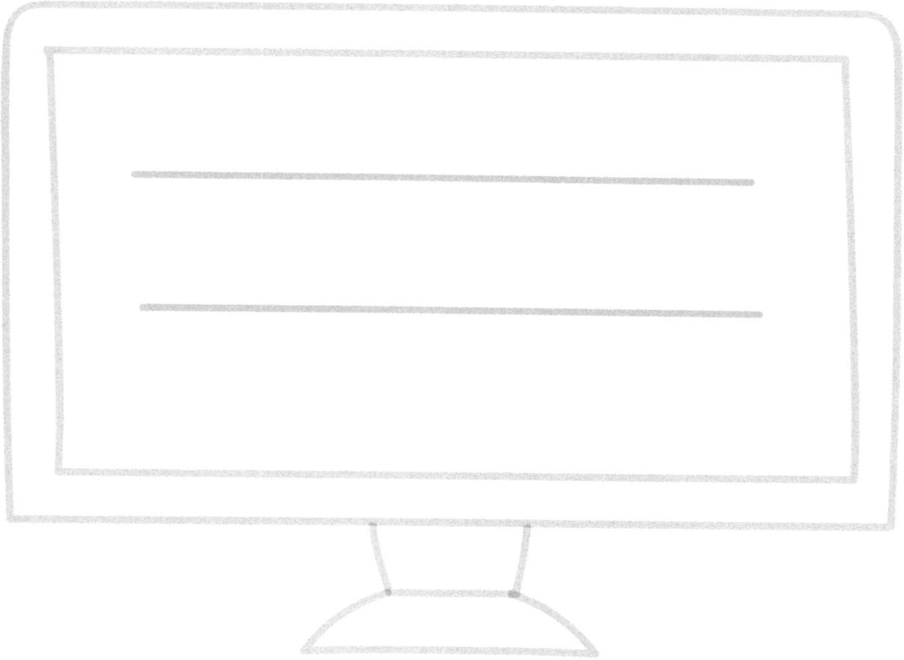

SCHOOL DAZED PRESS

I'm a teacher.
To save time,
let's just
assume I'm
always right.

[illegible]

[illegible]

Made in the USA
Monee, IL
15 December 2022

21796543R00057